Devotional Thoughts for Youth

Devotional Thoughts for Youth

WALTER L. COOK

Nashville ABINGDON PRESS New York

DEVOTIONAL THOUGHTS FOR YOUTH

Copyright © 1975 by Abingdon Press

Library of Congress Cataloging in Publication Data

Cook, Walter L.
  Devotional thoughts for youth.
  SUMMARY: Quotations from the Bible are followed
by explanations of their application in everyday life.
  1. Youth—Prayer-books and devotions—English.
[1. Prayer books and devotions] I. Title.
BV4850.C585   242'.6'3   74-14607

ISBN 0-687-10600-1

Scripture quotations unless otherwise noted are from
the Revised Standard Version of the Bible, copyright-
ed 1946, 1952, and 1971 by the Division of Christian
Education, National Council of Churches, and are
used by permission.

MANUFACTURED BY THE PARTHENON PRESS AT
NASHVILLE, TENNESSEE, UNITED STATES OF AMERICA

For Karen and Robbie

PREFACE

"Have a good day!"

We may hear this expression from a friend when we stop a minute to exchange greetings. Just as we turn to go on our way our friend may call out "Have a good day!"

This book of meditations is for all who want the day to bring hope and cheer, well-being and fulfillment. The scripture verses at the beginning of each meditation suggest how God speaks through his Word to help make the living of our days a benefit to ourselves and others.

We can make each day a good day if we sing a song of praise to God (in our hearts if singing aloud annoys our friends), if we get off to a right start, and if we are daring enough to set out upon an adventure of the spirit.

Walter L. Cook

CONTENTS

BURST INTO SONG

SHIFT INTO THE RIGHT GEAR

PLUNGE INTO ADVENTURE

Burst into Song

Just a Bit Off-Key

Singing and making melody to the Lord with all your heart. Ephesians 5:19

A brother and sister called a friend on the friend's birthday to offer their greetings. They dialed the number and sang "Happy Birthday" into the telephone. But after they had finished singing (more than a little off-key) they found they had the wrong number. They apologized sheepishly.

"Don't let it worry you," said the Wrong Number, "both of you can sure use some practice."

Singing! Who does it anymore—except professionals and members of church choirs? We have grown so self-conscious that unless we are taking lessons and have been assured that we have a promising voice we seldom break into song. We may even be embarrassed to join with friends in singing "Happy Birthday." And if someone remarks that we're off-key, that does it: we never sing again, and begin to repeat the old wheeze, "I can't carry a tune in a basket."

The author of the book of Ephesians pictures bands of Christians "singing and making melody to the Lord" with all their hearts. Now those first

Christians were not all lyrical tenors and splendid sopranos. Still the Ephesians writer does not urge the discordant singers to apply the soft pedal. Rather, he encourages all to sing, the squawking crows as well as the tuneful thrushes.

Many preachers urge their congregations to respond with hearty "amens" during Sunday services. They also encourage worshipers to sing the hymns whose numbers are listed in the bulletin. But some Christians say, "I just can't sing a note." So they stand up during the hymn-singing, grip the pew in front of them, stare at the cross on the communion table and wait, without once opening their mouths, until they can sit down.

Most of us make better melody in our hearts than with our voices. At any rate, our best days are singing days, days when we lift hearts and voices in praise to God.

O Lord, help us to begin and end each day with a song, a song of praise to thee that comes from our hearts. Amen.

Gifts That Startle

And behold, a woman of the city, who was a sinner, when she learned that [Jesus] was at table in the Pharisee's house, brought an alabaster flask of ointment, and standing behind him. . . , began to wet his feet with her tears, . . . and anointed them with the ointment. Luke 7:37-38

The catalog of one of America's largest department stores once made an unusual suggestion for Christmas giving. It advertised a live steer for sale and promised to send it "gift-wrapped as best we can."

To receive a steer by parcel post might startle us a bit, even though Christmas often produces its quota of surprise gifts. What could we do with the beast? He would be a size too large to tie under the lighted tree. Our thank-you note to the giver might read: "Thank you for the steer; come by some day soon and enjoy a hamburger steak with me."

But just the same, do we not admire some acquaintance who shows lively imagination in the gifts he chooses for friends? The fellow may not have much money, but the originality of his presents is as beguiling as if he had spent a fortune upon us.

15

The Gospel of Luke tells the story of a woman who made an exceptional gift to Jesus, a flask of expensive perfume. Some bystanders who witnessed the act of giving were stunned when she broke the flask and anointed the feet of the Master. The formal surroundings, the woman's impulsive deed, the delicate scent spreading through the room—these united to make an extraordinary impression.

Do our own gifts to others seem colorless? Perhaps we would like to give abundantly to our family, close friends, and several classmates. But the lavishness of our gifts is not important; it is the thought and care we put into the giving that makes them valuable.

It is good to give graciously to our friends; it is even better to give freeheartedly to God. The best gift we can make to him is that of our lives in his service; lives that are wrapped in obedience to his commands and sealed with day-by-day dedication.

Grant, O Lord, that we may find joy in our giving. May the generous sharing of our possessions become a habit with us. Amen.

Surprised by Gladness

And the shepherds returned, glorifying and praising God for all they had heard and seen. Luke 2:20

According to a fable a puppy said to a big dog: "I have mastered philosophy. I have learned that the best thing for a dog is happiness, and that happiness is my tail. So I am chasing it. When I catch it I'll catch happiness."

Said the older dog: "I too believe that happiness is a fine thing for a dog and that happiness is my tail. But I notice that when I chase it, it keeps running away from me, yet when I go about my business it comes after me."

Can *anyone* catch happiness by chasing it? Perhaps the fathers of our country thought so when they declared that all citizens are entitled to "life, liberty, and the pursuit of happiness." They believed all should have the right to seek happiness, but they made no promises that seeking would always mean finding it.

Happiness is something we stumble over when we are doing what we ought to be doing. That happened to the shepherds in the story of the first Christmas. On the night Christ was born they were not trying to catch up with some great joyfulness. Rather they were guarding their sheep

—just what shepherds are supposed to be doing. Then while they were at work they got the most happy surprise of their lives: they learned of the birth of Jesus. And after their visit to the manger they went back to work "praising God for all they had heard and seen."

When we go looking for happiness we are on a fool's errand; we will never find it. But there is a good chance, although it is not guaranteed, that when we are doing what we are supposed to be doing we may be astonished by joy. While focusing on our studies, buckling down to our part-time job, or giving a younger sister or brother encouragement and support—just what we should be doing—great happiness may invade our lives.

Almighty God, if today while we are at work some unexpected blessing or unlooked for happiness should break in upon us may we be thankful. Amen.

If You Want to Be Free

And suddenly there was a great earthquake, so that the foundations of the prison were shaken; and immediately all the doors were opened and every one's fetters were unfastened. Acts 16:26

Years ago an inmate escaped from a Maryland prison through a tunnel that had taken him two years of continual risk and hardship to dig. He loathed the walls that shut him away and sealed him in; he hungered for freedom.

All of us hate ropes, chains, handcuffs, and prison walls that plunder our liberty. Like the prisoner digging and digging in the tunnel we crave freedom. Probably few of us will serve time, but this does not mean that we shall remain fully free. There are other kinds of fetters that hold us captive, fetters which are just as binding as the doors of any federal penitentiary or county jail.

Time and again Almighty God has acted to set free those who are in chains. The story of Paul and Silas gaining their liberty is only one example of how God's power can strike off chains that bind. These valiant men had been thrown into prison unjustly. Their deep faith in God had got them into trouble. But he did not forget them. One night as they sang hymns and prayed, an earthquake

19

shook the prison; its door flew open and their fetters fell off.

Many today are held in chains by fretful temperaments and ugly prejudices. Others are prisoners of drugs. Still others are addicted to habits that drag them down, destroying their self-respect.

There are days when they yearn to be free; when they must feel as the prisoner felt who put all his strength into an effort to escape.

Just as Paul and Silas were set at liberty through the power of God, so today if we will put our trust in him, he will loose our shackles and set us free.

Almighty God, give us the strength of will to break loose from evil habits and binding prejudices that we may be free. In the name of Christ our Lord. Amen.

The Art of Saying Thanks

Then one of them, when he saw that he was healed, turned back, praising God with a loud voice; and he fell on his face at Jesus' feet, giving him thanks. Luke 17:15, 16

A young man was critically ill and needed a blood transfusion of a special type. A donor was found who was willing to give the blood the boy desperately needed. When he had recovered from his illness the boy wrote to the blood donor: "How can I ever thank you for what you did for me! I owe my life to you."

The boy's heart was brimming with gratitude but he had to confess he couldn't adequately express his thanks. Still, his letter showed that he tried.

Gratitude is one of the most praiseworthy qualities of character. In these days when so many of us disregard, or take for granted, the assistance that others have given us, a thankful heart is as refreshing as it is rare. If we are not thoughtless we will remember gratefully parents, neighbors, and teachers who have given us many a lift.

Once a man healed of leprosy by Jesus expressed fervent thanks for his restored health. With nine other men suffering from the same terrible affliction he came to Jesus for help. And as always

21

when the ill and suffering appealed to Christ he gave them his help. Nine went off about their business and never bothered to praise the Lord. Just one turned back to Jesus, "and fell on his face at Jesus' feet, giving him thanks."

Tomorrow or maybe later today we may be granted a special blessing from God. Or perhaps we shall receive some kindness from an acquaintance; a classmate may invite us to an exciting party; a neighbor may surprise us with a small but choice gift; our employer may give us an unexpected bonus. Surely we will be grateful.

If we are let us say so.

Lord God, who has given us so much, give one more thing: a thankful heart. Through Christ the Savior. Amen.

How Much Do You Weigh?

He was a burning and shining lamp, and you were willing to rejoice for a while in his light. John 5:35

A fat man was walking along the street of a seaside town when he noticed a weighing machine with a sign over it which read, "I speak your weight." He put a penny in the slot indicated and stood on the platform. A voice announced, "One at a time, please."

We might ask ourselves: "Am I a heavyweight or a lightweight in the strength of my convictions and in my capacity to think deeply and think straight? Do my convictions carry weight with others because they know I am sincere and resolute?"

Individual men and women have often exerted a powerful influence on the lives of others; they have attacked half-truths and lies with such force that they seemed more like an army than individuals. When they stepped on the scales of public opinion their principles weighed a ton.

One of the exciting personalities of the New Testament story was John the Baptist. Jesus admired him and once said that John was a "burning and shining lamp." John was very much by himself, living alone in the wilderness and depending

23

for his vitamins on a most unusual diet of bugs and honey. But no matter how irregular his eating habits, he was fiercely righteous, and when he was scheduled to give an address he commanded a large and alert audience. His word carried more weight than the words of a dozen ordinary men.

Some of John the Baptist's descendants are alive today. They are the people who, when they are committed with all their hearts to high principles, will stand alone for those principles against a sea of opponents.

One man or one woman, powerful in conviction and strong in will, can still make a vast difference in our world.

Almighty God, grant that the influences coming from my words and acts may be for the good and never to the injury of others. Amen.

When You're Bored to Death

I lift up my eyes to the hills. From whence does my help come? My help comes from the Lord, who made heaven and earth. Psalm 121: 1-2

Many years before the development of agricultural machinery men were hired to cultivate by hand vast stretches of corn, beans, and turnips. For what seemed endless weeks a young man might be required to work alone in a field hoeing, hoeing, hoeing. Some found this a terribly dull job. One young fellow said that now and then he would look up from his hoeing to gaze at a range of far-distant mountains.

How we wish we could escape the dry and barren acres of routine living! Often our studies seem hopelessly dull, the teachers' assignments devoid of interest. Then again, our part-time work can be less than thrilling. Daily monotony holds us fast. It is hard to understand why tedious tasks seem so settled a part of day-by-day living.

But we need not plod through the days with heads down hoeing row upon row. The young man who found refreshment while looking at distant mountains had discovered some deliverance from boredom. He was a spiritual descendant of the psalmist who wrote, "I lift up my eyes to the hills."

Although much help will come by looking to the hills, even more will come from the Lord who made the hills. The psalmist said: "I will lift up my eyes to the hills. From whence does my help come? My help comes from the Lord, who made heaven and earth."

Indeed, getting our eyes up from the flatlands where dullness and drudgery and boredom prevail so often to high ground will add new life to our spirits. But a greater lift will come from the Lord who created the mountains.

A young girl once prayed, "O Lord, especially help those who have no mountain views in their lives." What about us? Have we some far horizons, some mountain ranges, that can change a dirge into a song?

Our Father, may we find friendship with you a source of lasting happiness. Amen.

Nothing Inexpensive About Me

What is man that thou art mindful of him, . . . Thou hast made him little less than God, and dost crown him with glory and honor. Psalm 8:4-5

In the Franklin County Court House in Virginia there is a tattered will of the man who once owned Booker T. Washington, the great American Negro educator. Most of the owner's property was in slaves; and beside the names of the slaves he had set down the price of each. Beside the name of Booker Washington he had marked two hundred dollars!

Imagine a price tag hung on any human being, be he black, yellow, brown, or white! The writer of Psalm 8 would not think of decorating any man with a sign estimating his worth in dollars and cents; nevertheless the psalmist did calculate man's value in another way. He said that man was made a "little less than God," and was given dominion by God over all God's works.

"A little less than God"! If we are tempted to belittle any human being at any time let this verse ring through our minds. If we grow to dislike some acquaintance so bitterly that we growl to ourselves or to our friends: "That so-and-so, he

27

doesn't even belong to the human race," we might think of the psalmist's striking phrase.

Probably there has never been a greater word-tribute paid to man—and this means any man, woman, or young person on earth—than is paid to him in these words. It *is* hard sometimes to believe that such an exalted estimate of man includes all our rivals, our critics, and our enemies. But it does.

The writer of this psalm lived many years before the days when Jesus healed and taught in Nazareth. But Jesus also underlined the value of man; in fact he thought so highly of man that he was crucified for him. Jesus' sacrifice for us all is the ultimate proof of man's worth.

We thank you, O God, that all mankind stands high in your sight. Ever keep us, we pray, from belittling any of the people or the things you have created. Amen.

Are You Missing Something?

Then Elisha prayed, and said, "O Lord, I pray thee, open his eyes that he may see." II Kings 6:17

Have you ever stood on a coastal cliff and gazed out to sea? Although you could discern a few things in the distance—a buoy, a small ocean-washed island, a seaplane skimming over the water's surface—there was something out there you could not see. Not until a friend came up and handed you his field glasses did you discover a sailboat far, far out on the horizon's rim.

Your natural eye was limited, but by the aid of binoculars the white sail came into view.

Limited vision was the problem of a young friend of Elisha's. The two men were surrounded by enemies and the young fellow panicked. But Elisha with his eyes of faith could see assistance that was not visible to the boy. So Elisha prayed: "O Lord, I pray thee, open his eyes that he may see." The Lord opened his eyes and he saw that "the mountain was full of horses and chariots of fire round about Elisha." Then he knew his deliverance was at hand.

Without the aid of Elisha to sharpen his vision the young man could see only a host of enemies. And he was terrified. But Elisha with eyes of trust could see escape from peril. He was not blind to the foes bent on destruction, but his eyes were also open to the armies of the Lord that had come to the rescue. Elisha was able to see the unseen. Like the young man, many of us are nearsighted; in everyday living we are not able to see that God himself can bless and help us. All we seem to see are troubles, pressures, and hardships. But just as a friend aids our vision on the seacoast or on some mountain top by handing us his field glasses, so trust in God and faith in his power can open our eyes to ways we can win victories over many ordeals. We need never panic about today's perplexities or tomorrow's misfortunes.

O God, our Father, whenever life seems to close in on us, give us such faith in your power that we shall not be dismayed. Amen.

No Hiding Place

Three times I have been beaten with rods; once I was
stoned. Three times I have been shipwrecked; a night
and a day I have been adrift at sea. II Corinthians 11:25

A medieval monk named Simeon tried to avoid
the evils of the world by sitting on top of a high
pillar. He drew up his food and drink in a basket.
One day hundreds of years later a boy named
Anatole became angry because of fancied mis-
treatment by his parents. He put a chair on the
kitchen table and climbed onto it. In imitation of
Simeon he tried to isolate himself from his family.
They just laughed at him.

Of course some of life's difficulties are no
laughing matter. And how we do try to dodge
them! We look for a hiding place. Instead of cut-
ting a way through the obstacles of everyday living we try to climb out of their path and hide in
some pocket of isolation.

How very different was the apostle Paul. No
remote island of detachment for him! He plunged
into the thick of life. And he knew every time he
waded through some crowd to reach a platform to
tell the story of Christ that stones might fly. He
may have ducked a flying rock or two, but he
never shirked difficulties he met in telling that

story. Hear his report on the hardships he grappled with: "Three times I have been beaten with rods; once I was stoned. Three times I have been shipwrecked; a night and a day I have been adrift at sea."

And we think we have difficulties! Could any of them rival those of Paul?

It might be good for us, the next time we want to cut and run from some important task that bristles with obstacles, to remember Paul dodging stones, swimming to shore after three shipwrecks, escaping from robbers, suffering from exposure.

But ask him, "Paul, was it worth it? Was it worth it to endure all your trials in order to serve the Lord?"

With a song in his heart he would answer with a ringing yes.

O Father, with the help of your spirit may we face our problems bravely and resourcefully. Amen.

When You're About Ready
to Go to Pieces

By your endurance you will gain your lives. Luke 21:19

In a city in France a man was stuck with a thirty-two-room chateau he could not afford to repair and could not sell. After trying for several years to find a buyer, and after an inward struggle, he decided upon a desperate course. To dispose of his white elephant he bought 130 sticks of dynamite and blew it up.

But the man had given it up long before he blew it up. Perhaps if he had hung on a little longer, tried a little harder to sell it, he might have enjoyed victory rather than suffered defeat.

To the spent cross-country runner who somehow perseveres long enough to cross the finish line may come a signal triumph. One more hour of painstaking study may lead to passing a tough math course. One further, brave attempt to patch up a dispute between alientated friends may gain a reconciliation.

Endurance is often the quality of character needed for achievement in many kinds of Christian living. Hard-pressed Christians throughout history have persevered for their beliefs. In Luke's gospel Jesus speaks encouragingly to men and women of faith who were later to suffer violence and injury. He told them that for his sake they would be harassed by their own families, that they would be hated and oppressed by state authorities, and that some would be tortured. But he added: "By your endurance you will gain your lives."

In other words, "Don't quit, hang on a little longer until you clinch the victory." This is reassuring to any who are tempted to become dropouts from serving Christ.

Someone has said that when the news is good we go to sleep, but when it's bad we go to pieces. The man who blew up the chateau went to pieces and we can sympathize with him. But sympathy in his case, as sometimes in ours, was not so much needed as endurance. In our struggle to carry out God's will we can hear our Lord saying, "Outlive the opposition, triumph will come."

Give us, Father, not only the right convictions, but also the determination to survive all attacks upon them. Amen.

Misery *Needs* Company

Two are better than one, because they have a good
reward for their toil. For if they fall, one will lift up his
fellow; but woe to him who is alone when he falls and
has not another to lift him up. Ecclesiastes 4:9-10

When Hurricane Donna struck Florida a few
years ago roofs blew off houses, trees fell on cars,
power lines wrapped around hedges and fence
posts. One homeowner reported that it was really
a small thing that demonstrated the violence of
the storm. A squirrel came down the man's chim-
ney and took a seat on a chair in the living room.

It was a storm so bad that all God's creatures felt
the need of getting together.

What a pity that so often a disaster is needed to
bring us together to help and encourage one
another! But what a blessing that when disaster
does strike we then come to one another's aid!

The author of Ecclesiastes stresses the importance of companionship in time of trouble: "Two
are better than one, because they have a good
reward for their toil. For if they fall, one will lift
up his fellow; but woe to him who is alone when
he falls and has not another to lift him up."

The old saying that "misery likes company"
should be changed to "misery *needs* company."

35

The so-called loner misses the warm encouragement and support that come from association with classmates and neighbors. We all urgently need one another, and this is true in fair as well as in foul weather. Many young people who attend youth fellowship meetings in their churches are looking not only for recreation and worship but also for upholding friendships.

The next time we are in such a meeting we might look around to see whether a loner is present. To advance upon him with an aggressive air of "I'm out to be of service to you, boy," could turn him off. But to greet him warmly if he is standing alone, seemingly unnoticed, may lead to an interchange that will help him to feel at ease in the group.

O Lord, we thank you for friends and neighbors who give flavor and warmth to our living. Keep us alert always to those who seem by themselves. Amen.

Shift into
the Right Gear

Reverse, Revenge,
and a Busted Rear Fender

Do not say, "I will do to him as he has done to me."
Proverbs 24:29

A policewoman in a small town once told of hearing an elderly citizen in court offer this account of a traffic accident: "I was just settin' there waitin' for the light to turn green when this feller came up behind and run into the back of me. So I just shifted my car into revenge and slammed into him."

Don't we feel every now and then just like this cranky motorist? When someone puts a dent in our jalopy, or perhaps in our ego, we want to slam him back—but quick! The only thing that may keep us from shifting into revenge is the knowledge that we would hurt ourselves further by trying to get even. If a fuzzy-minded driver crimps our rear fender we would only add another crimp if we banged him in return. So we grind our teeth, squawk with pain, and—if the offender isn't too much bigger than we are—tell him off.

When tempted to give in to our desire for revenge, two scripture verses can leave us almost dizzy with their demands. One reads, "Repay no one evil for evil, but take thought for what is noble in the sight of all" (Romans 12:17). The other is equally bewildering: "If your enemy is hungry give him bread to eat; and if he is thirsty, give him water to drink" (Proverbs 25:21).

Too often we find it troublesome enough to aid our acquaintances or little-known neighbors, to say nothing of giving assistance to an enemy. We are so busy going our way and doing our thing that stopping to help even a pal is a distasteful chore. And as for befriending an enemy—well just forget it.

A little girl once prayed, "Forgive us our debts as we forgive those who are dead against us." Those who are "dead against us" may, above all, need our active good will as well as our forgiveness. Let us pray that God who forgives us will grant us the spirit to forgive others.

Almighty God, help us to add to forgiveness kindness and compassion. Amen.

It's Performance That Counts

Let us not love in word or speech but in deed and in truth. I John 3:18

Several years ago a motorist was stopped by a trooper and accused of drunken driving. He assured the officer that he was cold sober. When the policeman persisted in charging him with drunkenness the man got out of his car and walked a straight line in the middle of the road—on his hands. Case dismissed!

When the motorist did his best to convince the patrolman by talking he got nowhere at all. But where a lengthy argument and a useless flood of words failed, a simple *demonstration* of his soberness convinced the cop, and the motorist was soon on his way again. It's performance that counts.

The writer of I John knew all about Christians who worked much harder with their tongues than with their hands, and he plumped not for words but for deeds. He urged Christians to pour out good will on their neighbors and then put in this warning: "Let us not love in words or speech but in deed and truth." When it comes to gracious deeds for others in need let us put our muscle where our mouth is.

Some of us are like the sidewalk superinten-dents we notice gawking at, and talking about, the workers on a construction job. We're mostly talk. As for laying a foundation of kindly acts on behalf of a needy neighbor we have little taste for the work.

To go out of our way to do an errand for a crippled acquaintance, patiently assist a "slow" classmate with his math, or help a family next door to move heavy furniture after water has flooded their home—these call for action not talk.

Good will toward others is a matter of living service not just lip service.

Almighty God, so nourish all kindly impulses that rise in our hearts that these impulses may ripen into deeds. In the name of Christ. Amen.

Strangers Are People Too

Love ye therefore the stranger: for ye were strangers in the land of Egypt. Deuteronomy 10:19 (KJV)

An elderly lady who was quite lame was driving to see her doctor when her old car blew a tire. She was on crutches at the time. As she eased the spare out of the trunk a car pulled up and a man jumped out and went to work to help her. The lady learned he was on his way to work and remarked: "You really don't have time to help me."

"I don't have time *not* to help you," he said. "I just wouldn't have been able to do a job all day, thinking about passing you up."

How much really do we owe a stranger, someone we've never seen before and will never see again? Do we even owe him the time of day? A non-acquaintance who has fallen into one of life's ditches should be able to get himself out or else depend upon help from some of his own friends.

That seems so often to be our attitude. But it is hardly the way the people of ancient Israel were instructed to behave toward strangers.

Sometimes aliens wandered into the Hebrew community and settled there. They occasionally became victims of abuse and injustice, although oppressing them was forbidden. For the law

43

commanded respect and goodwill toward outsiders: "Love ye therefore the stranger: for ye were strangers in the land of Egypt."

And strangers in distress are entitled to our concern; strangers who are lonely or ill or who have been overtaken by accidents. Too often we don't want to be bothered about the plight of such persons. We may notice their misfortune and experience a twinge of sympathy for them, but we are too busy, too intent on some mission of our own, to take a helpful interest in them. Our attitude toward many a hapless stranger seems to be, "Well it's too bad, but really it's his tough luck."

Our Father, help us to respond obligingly to all who need our help whether they are friends or foes, or just strangers. Through Christ the Lord. Amen.

Dangers of a Swivel Tongue

Death and life are in the power of the tongue. Proverbs 18:21

Perhaps we believe that acquaintances who are big talkers are also big gossips. They seem to belong to the Fraternity of the Wide-Open Mouth, and we take for granted that they make a specialty of speaking evil and dropping slurring remarks.

True, some big talkers slander and blister with their tongues, but tongues need not be abusive or sarcastic. As the book of Proverbs makes clear, great good can come from talk as well as great evil. The writer of the book says, "Death and life are in the power of the tongue."

Good use of the gift of speech may be the best way to make our lives helpful to others.

Perhaps we have no capacity for entertaining our friends and neighbors by rendering enchanting melodies on guitar or violin; and we cannot draw or paint diverting pictures that will please and amuse them. We really feel that ships carrying cargoes of talent did not enter our port. But we can talk, and the power of the tongue is almost without limit.

Suppose that someone were to hide a recording instrument on our person so that, unknown to us, all the words we speak for a month could be recorded and at the end of that time played back to us. As we listened to ourselves would we wince with shame? How many of the words coming off our swivel tongue would be harmful to others?

Surely *some* of our speeches would be helpful. As we listened we might get an understanding of just how much blight a tongue can bring. And we might also see how a kindly tongue can put heart into a despondent friend, help to replace gloom with cheerfulness in some classmate's day, and cause a member of our family to live the rest of the day with fresh courage.

O Lord, may bracing and refreshing words be often on our tongues. In Jesus' name. Amen.

What Does Your Mirror Do for You?

He who belittles his neighbor lacks sense. Proverbs 11:12

Looking at the old family albums has been a favorite pastime of the young people in our home. They study some of the old-fashioned dresses, odd-shaped cars, unpaved streets, and an ancient record player with its immense horn, and then they laugh and laugh.

A neighbor of ours has the most antique collection of snapshots I've seen. One night he had the old album on his knee and was turning its pages when a visitor dropped by. The visitor laughed uproariously at the pictures. They just about broke him up. But on the way out of the house the caller stared a moment at his own face in the hallway looking glass without so much as a grin.

Many of our acquaintances these days seem so strange. They look strange, say strange things, have queer prejudices, the oddest hangups. They get uptight about the most ridiculous opinions. You just have to face it: an awful lot of quaint people are walking about. They look funny, really funny.

Too often we belittle acquaintances who seem

"different." Granted, certain intimate snapshots of our remote ancestors are droll, and some people we see every day make us want to laugh, yet a few consultations with a looking glass should cool our merriment at others' expense.

Do we suffer sometimes from a dislocated sense of humor and laugh at the wrong things: people's handicaps, their protruding noses, their knock-knees, their retarded responses to our sparkling wit, their awkward athletic performances?

It was a wise man of long ago who said: "He who belittles his neighbor lacks sense." To ridicule a neighbor, make light of his good qualities, and pull to pieces his opinions does not prove how keen we are but how immature we are. Actually, we are not even on the road to maturity until we have learned to laugh heartily—not at others—but at ourselves.

O God our Father, grant that today and all other days we shall neither scorn nor ridicule the opinions of others. Amen.

What's That in the Center?

But every nation still made gods of its own, and put them in the shrines of the high places. II Kings 17:29

A few years ago a professor in a large university said that a football should be gold-plated and placed on the communion table in the chapel.

How come? What provoked such an outlandish suggestion? "Well," explained the professor, "in this school a football is the chief object of worship."

Before we find fault with those who make gods out of footballs, baseballs, basketballs, or water skis we might ask ourselves what *we* would put on the altar as the center of our devotion?

The writer of the II Kings warned the nations not to make gods of their own to put in their houses of worship. That writer lived many centuries ago, but his warning is as up-to-date as this morning's news bulletins.

Just as nations made their own gods so do we as individuals. If we do not bow before the football or basketball god perhaps we do fall down on our knees before some other god. Would we perhaps put a crisp one-hundred dollar bill at the center of our worship? Or maybe we would reserve our homage for something less tangible than athletic symbols or bank books; it could be that fame or prestige or popularity have become our gods.

We sometimes accuse others of being "self-centered." Could we ourselves be accused of the same thing? Perhaps if we were wholly honest we would admit that the center of our worship, there on the altar or communion table, is a photograph of ourselves. *Self* may be the god we really worship.

Centuries ago in a voice of thunder Almighty God laid down this law: "You shall have no other gods before me" (Exodus 20:3). Now, in our day, we are still commanded to bow down before one throne only, to obey but one voice, that of the true God made known to us in Jesus Christ.

Father, you are the true God. We would worship only you. Every day may we be alert to your guiding voice and deaf to voices that call for loyalty to false gods. Amen.

Nobody's a Bum

Honor all men. I Peter 2:17

While he was riding on a city bus a man pulled out a cigarette and lighted it. An elderly lady was seated beside him knitting. When the first puff of smoke drifted into the woman's eyes she just shook her head and said nothing. But as a draft carried every mouthful of smoke in her direction she pointed politely to the No Smoking sign and asked him to stop. The man paid no attention. The lady reached into her knitting bag and took out a pair of scissors; then while the smoker was gazing out the window she snipped off the lighted end of the cigarette.

What follows here is not a lecture on the dangers of smoking. What does follow is an effort to call attention to the importance of genuine and neighborly courtesy.

The gracious Christian should practice consideration toward his fellow humans whether they are rich or poor, respectable or down-and-out.

Two men were speaking of an acquaintance. "Oh him! He's a drunk," said one of the men. But that "drunk" is also a person. To his wife, to himself when sober, and to Christ he is a man and a member, with all of us, of the human race.

51

The author of I Peter lays a charge upon Christians: "Honor all men." These three short words emphasize that we should respect others. He does not command us to agree with all men, pay court to all men, venerate all men, or adopt the practices of all. The word "honor" simply means respect for the humanness of all who live on the planet. God requires that we acknowledge the personhood of our fellow creatures whether they are distinguished public servants or the people next door.

O Father, we remember how Christ gave himself for us all. Remind us that not a single human being is worthless in thy sight. In Jesus' name. Amen.

Before It's Too Late

Train yourself in godliness; for while bodily training is of some value, godliness is of value in every way as it holds promise for the present life and also for the life to come. I Timothy 4:7-8

A blind horse provided the power that ran an ancient cotton mill. Week after week, month after month, the horse walked in a circle thirty feet in diameter. When, after several years of work the animal was put out to graze, he walked in circles of the same circumference as when he pulled the machinery of the mill.

The horse had walked in a circle so long that when at last he was free to walk as he pleased he continued in the same old way.

What are we doing now that will bind us in the future? The practices and customs of today may become the hidebound habits of tomorrow. The kind of interests we indulge now may harden into the interests that absorb us all our lives.

To be sure, people sometimes manage to break stubborn habits; but many of us will continue in the life-style we adopt when we are young.

It has been said of Aaron Burr, who killed Alexander Hamilton in a duel and was later tried for treason, that "all his life he was setting the stage for his final tragedy." The traits of character that

53

brought on his ruin became second nature by the time he was a man. There came a day when he could not break out of the circle of his old ways. Burr learned to his sorrow that the chains of habit were too weak to be felt until they were too strong to be broken.

Fortunately not all circle-traveling is bad; not all habits tie us to ruin. It is possible to root our lives in healthful and constructive habits. "Train yourself in godliness," says the writer of I Timothy. If we follow his counsel our lives will be made up of helpful and not harmful habits.

Almighty God, give us we pray, strength to form those habits now which will give depth and fullness to our future lives. In the name of Christ. Amen.

The Art of Quieting Down

Be still, and know that I am God. I am exalted among the nations, I am exalted in the earth! Psalm 46:10

A lady consulted her physician and talked so tiresomely and incessantly about herself and her complaints that the doctor could not give her information about her ailment. Finally the busy man exclaimed, "Put out your tongue, madam." After she had obeyed he snapped, "Now keep it there until I'm through talking."

The woman was a non-listener—just like many of us.

To be silent seems a great hardship, for we are all too eager to rehash our prejudices, report on our troubles, and brag about our victories. We often use our friends as sounding boards for our egos.

Then too, keeping quiet in the presence of God is usually difficult for us to contrive. We "go to God in prayer" and do all the talking, telling him about our wants and disappointments, begging for his approval of our plans for a successful future.

We are like workers in a boiler factory: we become alarmed during a few moments of quiet.

The psalm-writer relays advice for all who

storm the throne of God with pleas and plans and protests. God counsels us to "be still, and know that I am God." Prayer is not only a tongue talking to the Almighty God, it is also an ear listening to his voice.

Being "still" means more than simply deactivating the tongue; it is seeking out a place that is quiet and free from the clatter of everyday living and maintaining there an openness toward God. Water-skiing is exciting; snowmobiling is exhilarating; roaring down the pike in a low-slung sports job is invigorating. But all these activities, stimulating as they are, cannot provide lasting satisfaction; every now and then we should "get away from it all," be quiet, listen.

Almighty God, teach us that we can learn your will for us only as we listen to your voice. In Jesus' name. Amen.

Suppose We Are Being Followed

And he saw a poor widow put in two copper coins.
And he said, "Truly I tell you, this poor widow has put
in more than all of them." Luke 21:2

For five hundred dollars a New York photographer will follow you for two days, filming your everyday life at home, school, work, and recreation. She will then condense her pictures into a twenty-minute documentary movie—in color.

Can you imagine that any of our friends would like to review, over a soft drink, such a film of our lives?

Probably we would say: "How foolish to make a movie of what *I* do in a day, or two days, or a month! I don't do one thing important enough to be filmed."

We could be all wrong about that. Acts of ours that seem of little importance may be of real worth. Once Jesus commended a woman for an act she probably believed deserved no notice at all. He happened to observe her gift to the temple treasury. It was certainly a trifling one, a couple of copper coins worth less than a cent. But Jesus saw beyond the small gift to the woman's large heart. What he saw was a generous spirit and her willingness to give all she had. In commenting on her donation he said that she put in more than all the wealthy who were drawing on their riches yet never feeling the loss of their contributions.

Our Lord is not interested in the size of our contributions but in our openheartedness. What would a photographer discover about us if he focused on our daily routine? Would he find us taking time to greet cheerfully an elderly neighbor, or to help a little boy free his kite caught on a tree limb, or to give a classmate an opportunity to talk out his discouragement to us?

If a photographer should follow us about for two days to observe how we use our limited funds and scraps of talent he might form an opinion about our fitness as Jesus' disciples.

O Father, we have little money and less ability. Yet may we give freeheartedly what we have. Amen.

The Story of Our Lives

Then he poured water into a basin, and began to wash the disciples' feet, and to wipe them with the towel with which he was girded. John 13:5

A teacher assigned a Father's Day composition to her class of third-graders. A youngster passed in the following evaluation of Pop: "He can climb the highest mountain or swim the biggest ocean. He can fly the fastest plane and fight the fiercest tiger. My father can do anything. But most of the time he just throws out the garbage."

What a comedown—from flying planes and fighting tigers to emptying the garbage. And yet in a somewhat modified form isn't that the story of our lives?

In our dreams what daring and exciting things we picture ourselves doing! But the real picture is usually quite different. We "crawl out" in the morning, plod to school, maybe after school play a game of basketball at the Y, and come home to hit the books. Certainly nothing high-flying about that routine. And yet, such routine is necessary, for garbage has to be dumped and books hit.

While a young man, Jesus stooped to perform a most lowly task, even though many of the things he did seem to us exciting and dramatic. He was able to spellbind large crowds who gathered to hear him speak. He set forth parables that are considered the greatest in all literature. He healed scores of ill people, many of them desperately ill. But sometimes he even went out of his way to perform deeds that were far from colorful or dramatic. Just before his crucifixion he performed a most humble act: he got down on his knees after supper one night and washed his disciples' feet, dirty with Palestinian sand.

Let us never spurn humble tasks. Jesus washed his disciples' feet for a good reason: he was teaching them to undertake the role of servants.

In our homes, at youth meetings, at school we may be asked to help and serve. Even if the tasks have no glitter or drama still let us discharge them faithfully.

Lord Jesus, grant that we shall be willing to give ourselves in lowly service if it be your will for us. Amen.

Keep Off the Rocks

But follow righteousness, faith, charity, peace, with them that call on the Lord out of a pure heart. II Timothy 2:22 (KJV)

I have often speculated on what would happen if seamen in large ships tried, without the guidance of buoys, to get into some of the harbors along the Maine coast. Although many of these "dents" in our coastline look deep and wide, they are really shallow; often sandbars block entrance to all but the smallest boats.

Even safe harbors require bells and buoys that roll with the waves and signal their warnings. These signals have guided thousands to anchorage where they unloaded their cargoes. Without these markers, ships of imposing size would have run aground or foundered on jagged rocks.

Many of us who are landlubbers will seldom venture on the sea. But still we will need buoys to guide us in day-by-day living.

To steer a victorious course through life requires rules and principles. The author of II Timothy puts on record certain principles that will help to keep us off rocks and reefs. He says, "Follow righteousness, faith, charity, peace."

Years ago in England a young man was wasting

his life in foolish living. Gambling was his passion. One day he was converted to the Christian faith. From that time his life was guided by the very principles set forth by the writer of II Timothy. These standards were now his passion. He became a compelling influence for justice from the slave coasts of Africa to the plantations of North America. The most terrible evil of his day was the slave trade and William Wilberforce attacked that trade with all he had.

Let us take an inventory of our lives. What are the buoys—the principles—that are guiding us? The same standards that made Wilberforce a powerhouse for justice and mercy can guide us as well.

Our Father, so direct us that righteousness, faith, charity, and peace shall be the standards by which we live. Through Christ our Lord. Amen.

Outwitting a Faint Heart

My righteous one shall live by faith, and if he shrinks back, my soul has no pleasure in him. Hebrews 10:38

Long ago a dozen Christians arrived on a small island in the Atlantic. As soon as they had beached their boat they heaped earth and rock upon it and buried it. They had come to try to convert the islanders to the Christian faith. The natives were reported to be fierce and ruthless; the Christians were afraid. But their greatest fear was that they would become panic-stricken and would want to sail for home. So they buried the boat.

Some of the strongest people are those who know they can be weak. So they take their weaknesses into their calculations and prepare to overcome them. Such people know they had better "bury their boat."

Any Christian who is seeking to obey the commands of Christ may run into trouble. Jesus expects high-level loyalty of his followers. Some of his commands seem farfetched and foolish to non-Christians. Consequently the disciple who is trying to obey these commands may become the butt of ridicule and even hostility. He may grow fainthearted and want to turn back. Let us hope

63

that he will have buried the boat in anticipation of his cowardice.

"If he shrinks back, my soul has no pleasure in him." These words reveal God's displeasure with those who swear unflinching allegiance to him, but who falter and fail if they have to grapple with opposition.

Occasionally we say of a neighbor, "He's completely reliable, the kind of a guy who never lets you down." But some of the people about whom we feel most sure are the very ones who are least sure of themselves. They know full well they can fail to live up to the high standards they have set for themselves, and that only through prayer and daily fellowship with Christ can they live as his faithful disciples. Like the Christians who buried the boat they anticipate and prepare for times of weakness.

Help us, Father, not to back away from difficult and dangerous commitments when those commitments are in line with your will. Amen.

Pretty Good Is Not Good Enough

One thing I do, forgetting what lies behind and strain-ing forward to what lies ahead, I press on toward the goal for the prize of the upward call of God in Christ Jesus. Philippians 3:13-14

A famous coach, training the track squad of his university, found a muscular sophomore ear-nestly tossing the weight. Out in front of the ath-lete was a tall white stake planted a good 30 feet beyond his longest throws. "Is that really the mark of your best one?" the coach asked. "No it's not," said the ambitious fellow, never missing a toss, "that's the mark I've got to beat."

He hadn't reached it, but he was out to beat it.

Too many of us settle down reasonably satisfied with present achievements. "We're doing about the best we can," we say. And let it go at that. Are we afraid we will look foolish, aiming at some accomplishment that seems beyond our reach? Are we afraid of never reaching that goal so we just don't try any more? If we don't try, then we can console our egos by saying, "Well if I had tried I probably would have made it."

Many have refused to be satisfied with limited purposes. Paul the Apostle was one. His was a distant goal. He admitted that he had not attained

65

that goal but he said, "Forgetting what lies behind and straining forward to what lies ahead, I press on toward the goal." To share in the exalted life of Christ was his high purpose.

It is a tragedy when we stop growing, stop reaching, and cease striving.

If we had some sweeping victories yesterday, file them and revise tomorrow's goals upward. Have we forgiven all our enemies? Have we cut all hypocrisy out of our lives? Have we banished from our hearts all hate and bitterness and sullenness and evil desire? If we have not, then we still have some bases to touch.

Almighty Father, help me to spend this day chasing ultimate goals and far horizons. With the help of Christ. Amen.

Plunge into Adventure

Don't Back Off from a Dare

By faith Abraham obeyed when he was called to go out to a place which he was to receive as an inheritance; and he went out, not knowing where he was to go. Hebrews 11:8

An astronomer sweeping the sky with his telescope; a high school junior examining a spacecraft; a college student in a biology laboratory peering through a microscope fascinated by immeasurably small bacteria; a hiker following the Appalachian Trail over rolling mountains from Maine to Georgia; a truck driver deep in a book about the taming of the wild west; a youngster climbing far up the maple tree in his back yard —all these people are responding to one of the longings of the human spirit, the longing for adventure.

Thousands of years ago Abraham heard the call to adventure. He was inspired to follow God's leading. The scripture says of him, after he saw the beckoning hand of God, that he "obeyed when he was called to go out . . . and he went out, not knowing where he was to go."

How foolish can you get!

It sounds idiotic to begin a journey with no destination in mind. How foolish an airline pilot or a ship's captain would appear if they were bound for no terminal or port! And indeed it is true that usually we ought to know where we're going when we head out. But with Abraham it was different, for he went out in obedience to God's will. God said leave. And he left. Although the Lord listed no terminal or port for Abraham or gave even a hint about where he would be commanded to take up residence, Abraham was soon on his way.

Do we have a lively spirit of adventure which inspires a longing for cleaner, higher, more creative living? Let us not hold back from setting off on such a venture because we cannot see just where it will take us. Let us resist the temptation to back off from some grand experiment. The pull of adventure coupled with the determination to follow the guidance of God could lead to victorious Christian living.

Our Father, ever keep us alert to opportunities that will stretch our vision. Through Christ the Lord. Amen.

Medals for Doing Nothing

*And although she spoke to Joseph day after day, he
would not listen to her, to lie with her or to be with her.*
Genesis 39:10

Columbus gets a lot of credit for discovering a
New World. He ought to get just as much credit
for flatly refusing to turn back when his crew
threatened mutiny.

Washington is praised for crossing the Dela-
ware. He should be honored for repelling British
demands that he surrender.

Both men are applauded for what they did; they
ought also to be commended for what they did not
do.

The Bible tells about what great men and
women did, and reports also on what they did not
do. Joseph did many important things in Egypt;
he also refused to be seduced by his boss's wife.
Elijah swore allegiance to the one true God; he
repudiated the worship of idols. Moses led the
people of Israel out of Egypt; he rejected a life of
ease as grandson of a king. Nehemiah rebuilt the
walls of Jerusalem; he spurned making a deal with
a crook who tried to corrupt him. All these performed many good deeds; they also abstained
from evil ones.

71

Our Lord went about doing good things for people: he helped and healed, challenged and inspired, blessed and forgave. All this can make us glad. Let us be glad too that when he was tempted to join forces with the devil he resisted the temptation. During his ministry he turned a deaf ear to the petitions of his family and friends to quit his mission and go home to his carpenter's shop; and when his enemies ambushed him and delivered him to be crucified he never backed down an inch.

An American essay writer once said: "I like people who can do things." To be sure. Who doesn't admire positive achievements? But let us esteem those who decline to do evil, refuse to obey ignoble impulses, give in to corrupting influences, surrender to greed and lust and hate. Hats off to the guy who can say no to an enticing but sordid temptation.

Grant, Almighty God, that we shall be as prompt to rebuff the wrong as we are to support the right. In the Savior's name. Amen.

My Feet Are Killing Me

We who are strong ought to bear with the failings of the weak, and not to please ourselves. Romans 15:1

One day in a large city in the United States when surplus food commodities were being distributed, an elderly woman was too tired to remain on her feet as the long line crept slowly to the distribution counter. She stepped out of her shoes, left them in her place in the line, and went over to sit on a bench nearby. Those who stayed in line pushed her shoes along as the line moved until she got back her place by stepping into her shoes just as they reached the counter.

What would we have done if we had been next in line behind the woman's shoes? Would we have been tempted to kick the shoes to one side telling the woman, if she protested, "Stand on your own two feet the way everybody else has to."

People who cheat in a queue nettle us. We put them down as deadbeats. If some bumptious guy tries to wedge in ahead of us after we have been standing in line for a long while we bristle and growl. Many of us have a brightly polished sense of fair play—especially if we ourselves are victims of unfairness.

But if we are young and strong it is our duty to

be most indulgent of some feeble man or woman who leans upon our good humor, or seems to be trespassing on our rights.

The apostle Paul puts it this way: "We who are strong ought to bear with the failings of the weak, and not to please ourselves."

Consideration for others should be a preferred entry on our list of Christian graces. If we are husky and robust, then a generous quantity of kindly imagination is called for in our relations with all who are frail or infirm.

Inspire us, Almighty God, to make our rights and privileges secondary to our kindliness and good will. Through Christ our Lord. Amen.

Are We Chumps or Champs?

And thus Abraham, having patiently endured, obtained the promise. Hebrews 6:15

At Saint-Moritz in Switzerland a seventy-five-year-old bishop of the Anglican Church started skating early each morning and continued until dark. An observer of this remarkable sight asked the bishop's wife if she didn't think the all-day workout a little strenuous for him. "I suppose it is," she said, "but he does so want to be a champion skater before he dies."

Some people are like that; they just won't quit.

The aspiring—and probably perspiring—bishop endured tumbles, bruises, and much embarrassment but always got up and went at it again. His joints must have creaked and his breath come in gasps. Still he persisted. He "patiently endured."

The book of Hebrews tells about a determined, persistent man named Abraham. God made a promise to him that was not at once fulfilled. Nevertheless Abraham trusted God's faithfulness and at last obtained the promise.

The aged skater and the venerable Abraham both had a dream. Days came and went when they must have doubted whether their dreams could be realized. Still they could not shake off those dreams. Time passed, and although they struggled on, yet they seemed as remote as ever from their goals.

The list of great or near-great who have refused to abandon the pursuit of a purpose, a goal, a dream, would make a thick book. It is exciting to read of their struggles; and as we read we become convinced that only chumps give up; champs never quit. We might ask ourselves to which class we belong. When we pursue some far goal that seems beyond our grasp we may remember Abraham, who, having patiently endured, gained the promise.

O God, grant that we shall never become weary of working for high purposes and toward noble aims. Amen.

No Favoring Wind

From that time many of his disciples went back, and walked no more with him. John 6:66 (KJV)

One day years ago a little girl met a tramp as he was walking in a park. Thoroughly fascinated by this strange companion she asked him a question: "How do you decide which way to go?" With a gentle grin he replied, "I always travel with the wind at my back."

Daily living, to be really worthwhile, often calls for willingness to buck the wind, not drift along with it.

Remember how difficult and dangerous life was for the early Christians. For them days were never dull or flat. Just about anything could happen. When a man or woman joined a band of Christians at worship they soon learned that the place where they sang praises to God could be raided at any moment by Roman security police. If Christians traveled the trail blazed by Jesus, they would be facing a contrary wind.

Some of Jesus' disciples were delighted to accompany him when he was popular. A bit of the glory and applause he got rubbed off on them. It was just great! But one day "he set his face to go to Jerusalem," which meant he was soon to endure hardship, suffering, and at the end of his journey, a cross. When his half-committed followers learned that self-denial and privation were in store they "went back, and walked no more with him." They wanted always to travel with the wind at their backs.

These days tough decisions must be made about our life-styles. We cannot always afford to go along with the crowd when it seems to be drifting in the wrong direction—a direction that violates our deepest convictions. Anyone who earnestly tries to live a Christian life has to battle a relentless opposing wind.

Such a battle does promise an abundant reward: life never goes flat or gets stale.

O God our Father, ever help us to reject the easy way when it leads in the wrong direction. In the name of Christ our Lord. Amen.

On Getting Out of Jail

Bring out the prisoners from the dungeon, from the prison those who sit in darkness. Isaiah 42:7

Just a little while ago in New Orleans a sailor on leave from his ship was arrested for walking into a ten-cent store and releasing a dozen parakeets. He just opened the door to their cage and out they flew. The sailor exclaimed, "Come on out; I've been cooped up for months myself. I know how you feel."

Have you ever set anyone free, not from the county jail but from some prison just as confining?

Suppose you have an acquaintance who knows he has inflicted an injury upon you. You know it and he knows it. He is ashamed of himself and is held prisoner by his guilty feelings. By a word or gesture of forgiveness on your part you may set him free from his self-reproach.

Another acquaintance, perhaps a classmate, is a prisoner of loneliness. No dungeon is more grim than that of loneliness. Do we have the key that will let him out? Surely we can offer spoken or unspoken companionship to him in his dreariness. When we first approach him he may seem unsociable and so reserved that we doubt whether he wants our friendship. But if we make the effort we may turn the key that frees him from isolation.

One of our neighbors seems hateful all the time. He is a captive of hostility. At the slightest provocation he flares up, shouting angry words. A small irritation will set him off in a big explosion. Perhaps what he needs most is a friend to whom he may pour out his spiteful feelings. By listening patiently to the friend's outbursts, and perhaps acting somewhat as a target for them, we may help to set him free.

Once God told his people that they were to "bring out the prisoner from the dungeon, from the prison those who sit in darkness." We are God's people. Whom shall we set free today?

We pray, O Lord, for the guilty, the lonely, and the angry. Help us to do all we can to set them free. Amen.

Why Are We Hiding?

Whither shall I go from thy Spirit? Or whither shall I flee from thy presence? If I ascend to heaven, thou art there! If I make my bed in Sheol, thou art there! Psalm 139:7-8

A little girl stood on a kitchen chair, stretching as far as she could toward a shelf on which was a crock of cookies, a forbidden prize.

She looked around to make sure no one was watching. No one was. But on a wall was a portrait, the eyes of which were fixed upon her. She got down and moved her chair trying to avoid the eyes. No use. She tried another position. Still no use. Finally she climbed on a chair beneath the portrait and with a pencil stub punched out the accusing eyes. Then she contentedly ate half-a-dozen chocolate-bit cookies.

How to deal with a prickly conscience—that was her problem, and often it is ours.

When we feel our conscience sending us signals, what can we do? Well, we can ask ourselves honestly why all at once our conscience is making us feel guilty about a certain step we are about to take. It may be that conscience is warning us not to take this step because such an act would harm others or ourselves.

Just as some of us try to escape from the proddings of conscience so we seek to escape from the sight of God. The wise man who wrote Psalm 139 knew this was impossible; no one gets out of God's range of vision. We may sometimes feel that God through our conscience is accusing us. We should remember that on the other hand he often speaks to us in kindness; he is concerned for our welfare.

The real thing to remember is that there is no place to go from his spirit or flee from his presence. He has made us, and he will never let us go. If troubles harass us, he knows and cares. But if we stubbornly defy his commands, he will signal us by pricking our conscience. We cannot say, "God, get lost." He is ever close at hand to spur and guide.

Lord, may we never become dulled to the proddings of conscience. Help us to be sensitive to your leading in all that we say and do. Amen.

What Are We Looking For?

Now among those who went up to worship at the feast were some Greeks. So these came to Philip . . . and said to him, "Sir, we wish to see Jesus." John 12:20-21

A young man once found a five-dollar bill on the street. From that time he never lifted his eyes when walking. In the course of many years he accumulated 29,516 buttons, 34,172 pins, 12 cents, a bent back, and a miserly disposition.

For our part we will be fortunate if we never find a bill on the sidewalk or street; such a discovery might ruin us forever! What a disaster to go through all of life with a bent-over posture and a stingy nature.

If we are not looking for stray bank notes then what are we looking for? Some say they are looking for a scholarship that will pay their bills in a first-class college; some want a new color TV for their den (the old one produces too many distortions); others hope to win distinction on the athletic field; still others are certain that a car of their own will lend enchantment—if they can afford to buy gas for it.

So we go, forever searching for that which will bring happiness.

Whatever the goals we choose, let us beware of

ones that may produce a crooked spine or a greedy spirit. The Greeks who said, "We wish to see Jesus," apparently had been searching for the most luminous goal of all; they wanted to learn the truth about God. Perhaps their lives had been empty and their hearts heavy as they searched. Now at last they were looking in the right direction. Their days of collecting odds and ends of unsatisfying information were over. When they finally found Jesus they needed to go no farther. Now they could know God himself, because they had found Jesus the Christ, God's Son.

Today many of us ask, "Where is God?" We, like the Greeks, can find him in Christ.

O Father, keep us from wasting our days in a search for things that can never satisfy. Amen.

Someone Is Ahead of You

You became an example to all the believers. I Thessalonians 1:7

On a highway over the Rocky Mountains in Colorado a sign reads, "Millions have driven this highway safely before."

It has been no smooth, well-paved highway that many Christian heroes and servants of God have chosen to travel. Should not the lives of these dedicated people of God be to us a continual spur and inspiration? All of us who come after them can find their courage and commitment contagious. Because others have pioneered and blazed trails for God, we ourselves gain confidence that we can serve him too.

Once the apostle Paul wrote a letter to some church members commending them for being good examples to all who were seeking to serve Christ. Since then many more Christians have lived lives that can be examples to us. They have gone before, and our Lord commands us to follow their leading.

Surely we can find inspiration in reading the life story of a man like John G. Paton who went to the New Hebrides as a missionary. He had hardly begun his work there before his wife died in childbirth. With his own hands he dug the grave for his wife and baby, heaping pink and white coral above the grave. All but mad with despair and grief he persevered in his work and with Christ as his friend performed great service for his Lord.

Countless Christian men and women have traveled the road of suffering and have set for us an example of devotion to Christ that is all but incredible.

It could be that Almighty God is about to call upon us for a lifetime of service to him. If we answer yes to such a call we may not be able to see beyond the next curve what the road will be like. But we know this: Millions have driven that highway before us.

We thank you, God, for the faithfulness of so many of your servants. Grant that some of their faithfulness may rub off on us. Amen.

What Are We Fighting About?

I have fought the good fight, I have finished the race, I have kept the faith. II Timothy 4:7

An old fable tells about two fighting roosters, both very quarrelsome birds. One day they got into a bloody battle and fought so ferociously that they disabled each other; neither would ever fight a championship battle again. As the two roosters lay shattered in the dirt, a turkey who had watched the combat offered a comment: "How stupid you fellows were! You had no reason to fight except over some trifling thing like a morsel of corn on the path or just to defend your own silly pride. Now look at you, nothing gained and you're crippled for life."

Petty personal quarrels—how they sap our strength! And all for nothing.

Fighting over trifles with acquaintances and sometimes with friends disqualifies us for battles against injustice, greed, and prejudice that are so common everywhere. A savage tug-of-war over some minor matter burns up energy that could be used to attack the evils of the world.

Near the close of his life one of the early Christians exclaimed, "I have fought the good fight." Accent the word "good." Foolish fights are waged every day; there are far fewer "good" fights. Let us go into battle for noble ends and not give our time to battling for useless victories.

Why not go to war against ignorance, dishonesty, spitefulness, and hypocrisy wherever we find them? We know now that mankind can live in outer space and at the bottom of the sea. At the same time, on earth, day-by-day living is becoming more and more complicated. And the thing that is making living so tough is that too few fights—*good* fights—are being waged. When we come to blows with ignorance, dishonesty, spitefulness, and hypocrisy we will be engaged in battles that count. If we are winning battles against these enemies, then living on this planet will not be so tough.

Almighty God, teach us to choose the right enemies and then fight them until we win. Amen.

If You're Neither
Rich nor Clever

He looked up and saw the rich putting their gifts into the treasury; and he saw a poor widow put in two copper coins. And he said, "Truly I tell you, this poor widow has put in more than all of them." Luke 21:1-3

A youngster had but one ski, the other having been smashed when he slammed into a large spruce near the slope. All the rest of the boy's companions had the usual *pair*. A man stopped the lad and said, "Sonny, you ought to have two skis." The boy grinned at him, "I know I ought to have, mister, but you can have an awful good time on one ski, if you've only got one ski."

How important it is to make the most of what we do have and not to whine about what we don't have.

So often we hear someone say, "How I wish I had a pile of money, then I'd buy my friends expensive gifts. O brother, I'd sure spread the money around!" It really would be exciting to send expensive gifts to our friends. It would be great fun. Well, how much happiness are we enjoying right now with the dollar and a quarter we've got?

The poor widow in Jesus' story gave all the

money she could and received praise for her offering. All about her the fat cats were making huge contributions to the temple treasury. The best she could come up with were two copper coins. Jesus commented that she gave more than all others because she gave everything.

We may be discouraged not only by our short supply of money but also by our trifling talent. Our acquaintances may seem to have warmth and charm in abundance that can cheer and inspire others while we scorn our own flat-tire personality. Let us put to the test what aptitudes we do have, few though they seem. Even if we can offer but a small talent in service to God, we know it will be accepted. Let us never draw back from giving what we have in money and talent to him.

Keep us, Almighty God, from discouragement when we take an inventory of our abilities. Inspire us to lay what we do have on the altar of service. Amen.

If We're Just Drifting

One thing I do, . . . I press on toward the goal for the prize of the upward call on God in Christ Jesus. Philippians 3:13-14

"Ballooning is the only way for a gentleman to travel. No noise, no drafts, and you don't know where you're going. What could be better than that?" When the Royal Aero Club of London held its jubilee celebration, Lord Brabazon, holder of the first pilot's license ever issued in Britain, gave a television audience the above opinion on present-day air transportation.

"And you don't know where you are going."!

Lord Brabazon seemed to think that was the ideal way to travel, and indeed many these days do sit back and let the forces around them push them this way and that. Thus they are saved the necessity of making up their minds about anything.

Often such people pride themselves on their openmindedness. In some ways this attitude is praiseworthy. But it can also be dissatisfying to just shift into neutral and drift over acres of fuzzy opinions and jumbled bits of information and never commit oneself to a single all-engaging purpose.

If that is the way we are living these days we can understand the reply a certain well-known actress made to a friend who had just exclaimed to her in surprise: "Why, I didn't know you believed in astrology!" "Oh," said the other, "I believe in everything a little bit."

Compare this aimless wandering of mind with the driving force of the apostle Paul's commitment: "But one thing I do, . . . I press toward the goal for the prize of the upward call of God in Christ Jesus." And his daily living backed up his words.

Paul knew where he was going, and if he could speak to us today he would urge us to keep a certain landing field in mind in the form of an unswerving purpose; that purpose to be a lively response to the "upward call of God."

O Lord, give us a dependable sense of direction. Help us to bear down hard on great purposes. Amen.